PLAYING THE BLACK PIANO

ALSO BY BILL HOLM

Eccentric Islands: Travels Real and Imaginary
Coming Home Crazy: An Alphabet of China Essays
Faces of Christmas Past
Playing Haydn for the Angel of Death
The Heart Can Be Filled Anywhere on Earth
Landscape of Ghosts (with Bob Firth)
The Dead Get By with Everything
The Music of Failure
Boxelder Bug Variations

PLAYING
— THE —
BLACK
PIANO

BILL HOLM

MILKWEED ○ EDITIONS

Published 2004 by Milkweed Editions
Printed in Canada
Cover and interior design by Christian Fünfhausen
The text of this book is set in Bembo.
04 05 06 07 08   5 4 3 2
First Edition

Milkweed Editions, a nonprofit publisher, gratefully acknowledges
support from Emilie and Henry Buchwald; Bush Foundation; Cargill
Foundation; DeL Corazón Family Fund; Dougherty Family Foundation;
Ecolab Foundation; Joe B. Foster Family Foundation; General Mills
Foundation; Jerome Foundation; Kathleen Jones; Constance B. Kunin;
D. K. Light; Chris and Ann Malecek; McKnight Foundation; a grant
provided by the Minnesota State Arts Board, through an appropriation
by the Minnesota State Legislature, a grant from the Wells Fargo Founda-
tion Minnesota, and a grant from the National Endowment for the Arts;
Sheila C. Morgan; Laura Jane Musser Fund; National Endowment for
the Arts; Navarre Corporation; Kate and Stuart Nielsen; Outagamie
Charitable Foundation; Qwest Foundation; Debbie Reynolds; St. Paul
Companies, Inc.; Ellen and Sheldon Sturgis; Surdna Foundation; Target
Foundation; Gertrude Sexton Thompson Charitable Trust; James R.
Thorpe Foundation; Toro Foundation; and Xcel Energy Foundation.

Library of Congress Cataloging-in-Publication Data

Holm, Bill, 1943-
    Playing the black piano / Bill Holm.— 1st ed.
      p. cm.
    ISBN 1-57131-417-2 (pbk. : acid-free paper)
    I. Title.
    PS3558.O3558P55 2004
    811'.54—dc22
                                            2003016855

This book is printed on acid-free paper.

TO THE MEMORY OF

MIKE DOMAN, 1945–1991, and BILL "CUTZ" KLAS, 1933–2002, who practiced princely generosity to guests, to literature, to the liveliness and wisdom of the human spirit, who kept their fine old houses open to a little good whiskey and good talk late in the night, who left too soon. Salud, my friends!

PLAYING THE BLACK PIANO

III: FREE MARKET WIND

SPECIAL THANKS

No book is ever made without the wisdom and generosity of friends. I list them as the alphabet finds them. A thousand thanks.

John Allen
David Arnason
Kristján Árnason
Scott Beyers
Carol Bly
Robert Bly
Marcy Brekken
Emilie Buchwald
Phil Dacey
Leo Dangel
B. J. Elzinga
Daren Gislason
Tom Guttormsson
Einar Már Guðmundsson
Jim Heynen

Hu Zongfeng
Wincie Jóhannsdóttir
Charles and Joan Josephson
Les and Donna Josephson
Louise and Annie Klas
Adrian Louis
Gail Perrizo
David Pichaske
John and Lorna Rezmerski
Bart Sutter
Valgeir Þorvaldsson
Doris and Don Wenig
Phyllis Yoshida
Yu Dingman

PLAYING THE
BLACK PIANO

I

A BOWL OF THOUGHT

THE GHOST OF WANG WEI LOOKS
AT SKAGAFJORD

How the old Chinese poets would have admired Iceland!
Everything appears one at a time, at great distance:
one yellow wildflower, one brown bird, one white horse,
one old ramshackle farm, looking small and far away
with its polka-dot sheep and that ten-mile-long
black mountain lowering behind it. One farmer
the size of a matchstick walks out of his thimble barn
to his postage-stamp hay field while
over his head a river falls half a mile
off a cliff, a silver knitting needle
that disappears for the length of a finger.
Still you can see the farmer, even from this distance,
his tiny black boots, his brown coat, his blue hat,
his moustache, his slightly bloodshot eye
in which you can just make out the reflection
of the Atlantic Ocean and the whole sky.

BIRD POETRY ON SKAGAFJORD

Seabirds arrange themselves into a sentence on the water.
A crooked line of gulls and ducks
bob into the slow tide for breakfast.
Enough for everybody under here!

They are spelling something—a message
in white and gray, printed
on blue textured paper.
Much as I squint and mumble
to myself, it still won't come clear.

Every now and then, a letter or a whole
syllable takes off into the air,
rearranges itself in the dative case,
or maybe a plural. It seems
too certain to be subjunctive. The raven
punctuates the sentence.

This bird letter arrives
for me to admire,
but never understand.

IN THE SAUÐÁRKRÓKUR SUPERMARKET

I'm in a foreign country, a brightly lit supermarket with strange language, strange food, all wrapped in plastic: salt horse, smoked fish, ammonia shark, a black damp cube of rye bread, cold mountain grass pancakes.

I fill a basket, go to the checkout line, a regular housewife. The blond teenage checkout girl's skin is so pale and translucent the organs within are almost visible. I pile my food on the rubber belt; the computer whirs, adding up numbers—so many kronur for horse, so many for grass pancakes. I hand her VISA. She looks sad and hands it back, a little flurry of foreign language. I hand her MasterCard. Again she shakes her head sadly. Another—all no good.

The blond housewives behind me mutter. They are waiting—waiting with baskets of Bugles and Coke and cream for coffee. They haven't got all day. This supermarket grows stranger and stranger, a foreign country even I have never traveled—the kingdom of the poor. I am betrayed by plastic. 75 dollars between me and shame. 4,500 crowns, 50 pounds, 120 marks, 225 pesos, 900 kwai.

But wait! Here's a 5,000 note—cash, the hoarded cash of the poor, a crown or two kept in a cup until there's enough for bread, milk, salt horse, a pancake.

I pay—saved one more time from standing naked in church, throwing up on the president's shoe, leaving quietly by the rear door, moving on down the street wondering whether any bed on earth will let me lie on it tonight, or any quilt will give consent to cover me, at least until morning when I must leave before the others wake.

In the kingdom of the poor, every language is foreign, every country is strange, somewhere you've never traveled before, that will not want to see the likes of you again.

AT THE ICELANDIC EMIGRATION
CENTER IN HOFSÓS

Says the old Icelander
choosing carefully his English words:
"If it had been then as it is now
your grandfather would never have left."
"No," I nod, looking around the parking lot,
but think only silently: Give a man
a big Toyota, a cell phone, a debit card,
and he won't go anywhere.
"No, he would not have left," I say aloud.
"And I would have been born here
where I could have caused trouble
in Icelandic, and not English."
He thinks this is witty, so he laughs,
probably thinks I have inherited
Icelandic humor. What trouble
could anyone cause here
where trouble left so long ago,
leaving the open hole where money
could flow into the harbor like the tide
lifting all the gleaming boats
a little nearer heaven?

FOOD FIGHT DUET. SANICHTON, B.C.

for Louise Halfe and Lorna Crozier

In this genteel Canadian suburb
Cree and Icelander duke it out
over which morsels from nature
can be taken by mouth.
Says Icelander: "Pickled ram's balls, rotten shark,
sour seal flipper."
Says Cree: "Boiled moose nose, rabbit brains,
raw elk's liver."
Says Icelander: "I'll see your deer kidney
and raise you a cod cheek."
"Indian popcorn," says Cree.
"Fried chunks of bear fat—delicious!"
Icelander volleys back a shot:
"Dried stinky fish the texture of cardboard."
Cree slams it over the net:
"Ah! Moose cock jerky spread with gut fat!"
Torpedo-shaped carrots sit in a porcelain bowl
next to the green-flecked sour cream dip
as the food of the poor flies through the air
never bothering to land on a plate at all—
not a menu but an honor roll.

BREAD SOUP: AN OLD ICELANDIC RECIPE

for Disa and Einar

Start with the square heavy loaf
steamed a whole day in a hot spring
until the coarse rye, sugar, yeast
grow dense as a black hole of bread.
Let it age and dry a little,
then soak the old loaf for a day
in warm water flavored
with raisins and lemon slices.
Boil until it is thick as molasses.
Pour it in a flat white bowl.
Ladle a good dollop of whipped cream
to melt into its brown belly.
This soup is alive as any animal,
and the yeast and cream and rye
will sing inside you after eating
for a long time.

TJALDUR AT TJØRNIR

Outside the small farmhouse where
the old lady fries trout for lunch
while the clock ticks, and the three:
Kjartan, Kristján, and Sigrún,
all better than seventy, sigh and trill
about the fog that hides the fjord,
the cold summer, deserted farms;
the oyster catcher perches on the garden post,
settles his white-tipped black body,
surveys the fog with his fat red eye,
plants his pink feet and thweeps,
thweeps a hundred thweeps in a row,
same pitch, same duration, fortissimo,
like a stuck New York car alarm,
but the police do not come,
I do not applaud, his true love
does not join him in duet, the fog
does not part to unveil Tindastoll,
but he gives not a damn
about any of this, raises
his sharp orange beak that's twice
the length of his head, and like
a crazed jazz trumpeter, Satchmo
with one note, no hot licks, goes on
thweeping for no reason at all

that he's willing to divulge to me.
He's telling the sea fog something,
but it pays no attention either.
The trout is ready, says Sigrún, who
is so used to this one note serenade
that it must sound to her like the tune
the fog sings when it falls and rises.

BACH IN BRIMNES

Stebbi brings his cello into Brimnes.
He is a big thick fellow with ham fists,
Who looks like a seaman or a deck hand
More used to tubs of fish than cello bows.
No scores here, so he plays what he knows:
Bach! Let's have some Bach! Play a saraband!
The cello seems too big for this small room
But when he starts the Saraband in G,
The whole house grows too tiny for the tune,
As if the walls demanded to expand
Another fifty meters toward the sea
To make a proper space for all this sound,
If any human space at all could house
The planets whirling round inside this suite.

SUMMER LIGHT IN BRIMNES

A few miles from this window on the fjord
sits Drangey, the sheer-cliffed island where
Grettir the unlucky hero hid from law
but mostly from the dark.

When night came back to end the summer light,
Grettir swam four miles through freezing water
to find fresh fire after his lumpish servant
let the only embers flicker out and die.

The story's been told for seven hundred years
of this fierce man who fought trolls, ghosts, bears,
but was afraid to sleep without a fire
to burn away the specters in the dark.

Goethe, on his deathbed, said: "More light,"
and painted every room he wrote in white.
Almost old, I've come here to stay
the summer in this cottage without shades.

Here, whenever I roll over in my bed
and wake up in the middle of the night,
it is day, whatever any clock may say,
since my first sight is always light.

The solid world there to greet me,
water, grass, the island, sky,
just where I left them to sleep a while,
the illusion of eternity—

if not the fact. Like Grettir I depend
on darkness to arrive,
on whatever light I gather in to end;
however long a swim I make for fire.

ICELANDIC RECYCLING
ON A SUMMER NIGHT

for Wincie

Toward midnight, the sky pinks up.
The low cloud at the bottom of Tindastoll
turns the color of wild grapes.
Inside four women sit around a table,
oblivious to natural phenomena,
folding plastic bags
into neat white triangles.
"Ever so much nicer to store!"
They are performing women's work:
tidying up the garbage
until it looks like modern sculpture.
They have seen it all before:
midnight sun, revolution, disease, chaos.
Their female wisdom comprehends
there is nothing to be done about chaos,
except bring order and harmony
to plastic bags as if they were
wandering children needing to be tucked
in neatly for the long night.

NIGHT FISHING IN SKAGAFJORD

For three hours every night for a week
Little Valdís from across the road
Fishes by herself in the fjord,
Casting over and over again
Into the oncoming tide until
Midnight when her father comes
To fetch her fishless home.
What is she? Thirteen?
Black rubber boots, dark hair tied up in a tail,
Blue jacket, a bag for uncaught fish.
What does she cast for every night
In this white light that lasts 'til August?
Pink trout? Love? The future?
Or does she fish to practice patience?
Her back to the town, the world, my window—
Her face alone toward nothing
But the sea.

TO KRISTJÁN ÁRNASON

"I am a poet in words and wood,"
says Kristján Árnason at more than seventy
as he presents me with a wooden bowl
he has made at his house at Skálá,
a farm almost on the Arctic Circle.
In two thousand and one,
if you say in poem or song to your fellow man:
"This is a beautiful bowl," they laugh,
saying: "That is only your view, your denial
that trees have suffered, that one bowl
is necessarily more beautiful than
another bowl." They want an ironic
bowl, not a wooden bowl full of poetry,
but Kristján, a carpenter by trade,
never studied such fashionable stuff,
instead makes beauty from whatever
he finds at hand. He makes his poems
from whichever language he pleases,
bowls of words in English, Danish,
his own beloved Icelandic, which has been
filling bowls with beauty for a thousand years.
Here is a bowl of weather, a bowl of longing,
a bowl of mountains, a bowl of light,
a bowl of thought, a bowl of laughter.
A man does not study to make bowls,

or get a license or certificate.
He makes one after another until
they come right. Words, too, start coming
right if you make them every day for fifty years,
even on farms, so far from the world
of power and fame. Just as your bowl,
if you make it well, holds water
or pens or chocolate or agates,
so will your poems hold beauty
and wisdom and humor and love,
whatever language you make them in,
like the bowls of poems in words and wood
made by Kristján Árnason, skáld of Skálá
who made these gifts to me.

II

FREE MARKET MUSIC

ANGELS WE HAVE HEARD ON HIGH

On Christmas Eve monotones, duotones, or zero tones give themselves permission to bellow. You are expected to sing, the words are in front of you, you know the tunes, and besides, the Peterson boys blat away on out-of-tune trumpets to drown you out. So for one night, make a joyful noise.

My favorite carol, as a boy, was "Angels We Have Heard on High." It was French; it was operatic; it was half in Latin—just like the Catholics! It was not dour, slow, full of blood and lamenting; rather of angels singing, shepherd's jubilee and light, even the mountains "in reply, echoing back their brave delight."

And the chorus was not the standard Lutheran, one-note-to-one-syllable sensible plodding, but a glorious melisma of runs on the word *Gloria*—which sounded up through Scandinavian throats not as a word at all but a simple *Ahhh*—a singing for the act of singing alone—for the quivering in your own throat, for the air moving up in a great column through your body, from stomach, to diaphragm, to chest, to throat, to the bones of your face and out—out into the cold blustery Minnesota night like a tropical flower that said to hell with you all and bloomed in a snowdrift, filling the air not with chaste frost but with heavy sensual perfume of bodies with black hair and black eyes and heads thrown back and scales rolling out with no words at all, only the *Ahhh* of joy, pleasure, delight.

Now that was a hymn—but I was never so sure of the god's name praised there as the minister seemed to be. The god that deserved that Gloria did not worry about crummy presents, or getting ahead; that god threw open his mouth without squeamishness and let sound come out into the universe.

WHAT BEETHOVEN'S MUSIC
WILL DO TO YOU

Listen long enough,
you'll go stone deaf,
your body grow squat
from eating only
fish and brown sausages
washed down with hock.
Christen your sister-in-law
Queen of the Night, then
take her to court. Break
all the piano's strings,
howl and mutter and brood.
It'll do you no good.
He already wrote this music,
made it into the mirror
that always shows you
the back side of yourself
that you only imagined before.
Now you'll want to write
King Lear, paint *The Last Supper,*
rebuild the Parthenon.
That's how it always goes—
nose to nose with magnitude.

HEAVENLY LENGTH

Schubert does go on, doesn't he?
Don't you find him a bit much?
How much wine is enough
to wash down the bread?
Is there water enough to cover
the barges under Lake Superior?
Does the sun put out too much light?
Are there enough words
in the dictionary yet?
Too many teeth in the whale's jaw?
How many beautiful women
are too many? Will the men find them?
How much Schubert is too much?
Is it far from your left ear
to the top of the Greenland ice?
How many breaths do you intend
to breathe before you die?
Do you want these questions answered?
Someone is singing a long song.
Careful! It's getting inside.

THE MAN WHO THREW NOTHING AWAY

for Leonard Vader

My old friend Leonard believed in throwing nothing away, either
inside or outside except maybe Republicans and the lust for money,
so he stayed alive an entire eighty years. In America, some die at forty,
most by fifty or sixty, though they go on driving cars and expressing
opinions for decades while their visible graves, already lined with
concrete, await them and their goods. Leonard believed in healthy
chickens, proper gardens, rich compost, scrap lumber, the intelligence
of children, and that much in this universe can be fixed with duct tape
but little with money. He filled his garage with broken parts and single
gloves, because you never know when things might come in handy.

From one angle a small man, from another, he grew huge as he aged
by sporting a fine white mustache, never forgetting a story, and falling
in love every day till he was past eighty. The interior man grew heavier,
wiser, even happier, till the earth itself started singing loud songs to
beckon him down inside it. The earth wanted better company than
humans had been giving it lately.

On a fine damp Bellingham morning, Leonard went with a spade
to open his compost heap, his joy and visible emblem of the man
who saves everything. When he dug in, a cloud of fine steam billowed
up around his snowy mustache while the tabernacle chorus of the
compost sang to him in twelve harmonic parts of loud silence: Come,
from this we rise, to this we go, from this we come again. Inside our

rotting vibrant heart, your whole life churns and steams, waiting for you to join it. You have ripened like fine late grapes, full of unexpected sugar and flavor. Now it's time to become wine for a while. You saved everything to grow wise. Now it's time for us to save you for a century or two.

Two women who loved him took pictures of that steam and the look on his face that might even be transfiguration, but maybe only wryness, for he knew and they knew what others didn't, that once more, nothing is being thrown away at all.

PLAYING HAYDN FOR THE ANGEL OF DEATH

for Ethel Pehrson and Tomas Tranströmer

| 1 |

The piano tells things to your hands
you never let yourself hear from others:
Calm down, do your work, laugh,
love reason more, your mask less.
God exists, though not as church said.
To understand this language, you must
sometimes patiently play the same
piece over and over for years, then
when you expect nothing, the music
lets go its wisdom.

| 2 |

Play Haydn. First, when I was young
he seemed simple, even simpleminded;
too easy, too thin, too cheerful,
gaiety and dancing in a powdered wig;
no hammer blows at unjust fate,
no typhoons of passion dropping tears,
only laughter, order, invention,
the simple pleasure of ingenuity,
of making something from next to nothing.

| 3 |

All the geniuses have their own feel
inside the fingers. Mozart steps to center
stage, takes a long breath, then
sings his aria, but Haydn is skinny
under the hands; all the fat lives
in the spaces between the lines.
You sense that fat jiggling like
Buddha's belly but can't touch it.
After a while, you can hear it when
the notes pass lightly by each other.

| 4 |

But O, the mystery of Haydn is
the great reason for not dying young,
for living through rage and ambition
without quite forgetting their pleasures.
Suicide, craziness, the bottle, war—
all rob you of what is inside Haydn.
Take this advice: toughen up and live.
Fifty is a good year; by this time
something has probably happened, and with luck
it has tuned and readied the strings inside you.

| 5 |

At fifty, my own life has not come
to much and my death sits in

a straight-back chair under a lilac bush
in the garden behind my house,
reading my old letters, waiting.
He is in no hurry to come knock
on the back door. There's plenty to keep him
interested in the piles of my past
foolishness. Yours, too. On the other hand,
he has no intention of going
elsewhere, just wants to make sure
I notice him, every day, alert
in his straight-back chair.

| 6 |

Open the windows. Go to the piano.
Play a Haydn sonata for him. Begin
with an easy, simpleminded one:
Allegretto Innocente, just a tune
and a few variations, all in G,
the key of lessons for little fingers.
Haydn stays in it endlessly to see
what can be said with almost nothing.

| 7 |

Thirty years ago, I thought this
a trifle; now here I am playing it
for Death sitting in a straight-back chair.

You think he wanted Wagner maybe?
Or Schoenberg? Some dark thick Brahms?
What kind of idiot do you think Death?
If he can't hear what's inside Haydn,
how will he manage to throttle your heart?
That takes power, craftiness, patience.

| 8 |

Years ago, I wrote about Bach:
"Whoever loves G major loves God."
Truer than I knew, but I didn't say
quite enough: G major is one
of God's eyes through which he watches
hair go gray, or an ear that hears
the cracks in your own singing.
Remember, God and you have two of each
that watch and listen in two directions.

| 9 |

Has the angel heard enough G now?
G sings to life only half the earth
or half the truth. Go as far
away from G major as can be gone;
C♯ minor, the shadow, the nether tone,
but neither Ludwig's moonlight horsefeathers
nor Rachmaninov's gloomy thumping.
Too many wet sleeves and drooping heads.

| 10 |

Play Haydn where two gods have a civil talk
while they put the world together.
Haydn gives you two of everything:
two hands, two staves, two keys, two tunes,
two answers to all your questions.
What sits in the garden knows this.

| 11 |

For God *is* the imagination.
God made you up entirely, and you
have returned him the favor.
God imagined G major, C# minor.
Now, like Haydn, go and do likewise.
Make a surprise that stays a surprise
to please the ears and spirit of the one
who sits alert in the straight-back chair
under the lilac bush in the garden.

| 12 |

Having put the halves of the universe
back in order, it's time to dance—
a minuet, old-fashioned, but a dance
is a dance after all. You used to do
the minuet yourself, didn't you,
a few hundred years ago?

Remember the steps? Here's a good one:
Minuetto Giacoso in C.
You'll like the tune. Careful on the upbeat.
Put a lilac in your buttonhole.

| 13 |

When Haydn's own angel of death came
calling in Vienna, he found the old man
with worn-out wits, almost ready
to answer the door. But Death listened:
"I count my life backwards now,
and for a few moments I'm young again.
I ought to play for you. Do you want to hear
something of mine?" Then Haydn played, slowly,
Gott! Erhalte Franz den Kaiser.
His wet rheumy eyes glistened.
"I must play this song every day.
I feel well while I'm playing it,
and for a while afterward, too."

| 14 |

The world, though shriveled, remained in order
so Death stayed away for years,
sat on his street corner stool and listened.
Even Haydn could do no better
than playing Haydn to keep his guest amused.

As music drifts out the open windows
Death is dancing around his straight-back chair
under the lilac bush in the garden,
trying to make the left foot move in time.
Soon he will be tired out but happy;
he will nap a while and stay away.

That's the idea. I got it from Haydn.

ROMANCE OUBLIÉE. FRANZ LISZT. 1880

I

At thirty-two, Franz Liszt composes a full-throated love song, a
    Romance for the piano.
He is the handsomest man in Europe.
Women faint as he pulls off his tight white gloves, one slow finger at a
    time.
When he throws the glove away, ushers sweep down the aisle with
    smelling salts.
Then the piano sighs and teases, the energy inside the music grows
    until it swells and bursts into a volcano of singing.
Lava you can hear rises up against your body, first ankles, then thighs.

Afterward his cigar butts go home wrapped in silk, perfumed in
    lavender.
He inhabits the dream life of half-Europe for forty years.
The other half masks its closeted envy with public scorn, though he
    has locked his eagle talons on their dreams, too.
All the dreams but his own, in fact.
He dreams of God, Beethoven, solitude, even silence.

II

When he is seventy, a publisher asks to reissue his youthful *Romance*.
By now, he wears a priest's black cassock, and his old head is full of
    warts and wens.

No, he says, let the old one die. I'll compose it again, and try to say it
   right this time.
He breaks the tune into little pieces.
The old full-throated phrases end in the wrong key, then evaporate
   into silence.
He is stingy with his notes now, only a few, just a single line, then a
   single hand, then a single finger, then nothing.
No eruptions here; the lava cooled into slabs of obsidian, lit by
   flickering shadows.
The music threatens to disappear in a cloud of mist rising out from the
   strings.

III

Forgotten, he says, *Romance Oubliée,* yet he has forgotten nothing at
   seventy.
He has only learned more, felt more; knowledge arrived on his face
   along with warts and wens, with the deaths of children, lovers,
   friends, enemies.
The old *Romance* sank at the end into a minor chord because, at thirty-
   two, life is sad—wet and full of possibility.
At seventy, the *Romance* ends in a glowing major high up at the piano's
   summit.

What did he know at seventy that was invisible to him at thirty-two?
That nothing mattered in the way he thought it did?
That if you strike one piano string with one finger the vibration will
   travel out into the universe.

It keeps moving past the farthest star till it circles back to find the
    bottom of some keyboard
then works its way up the body past ankle and thigh until everything
    is connected again.

THE WEAVERS

for Don and Mim Olsen

They play a piano made entirely of string,
a tune of whirrs, and clunks, and ratchets,
the music gradually turning blue, gray, pink,
marked by diamonds, flowers and stars.

One passes a wooden shoe under the strings,
then clunks on her damper pedal.
The shoe goes back and forth, under and through.
It's the shoe of the invisible dancer
who pirouettes on one bare foot
somewhere inside the loom.
The choreography of her toes
weaves diamonds into the blue cloth.

In a thousand years
tapestry will turn into music,
marble into language,
colors into movement, and men
will all be reborn as women and give birth
to themselves over and over again
at a loom, weaving a shirt
to cover the breasts of someone they love.

"KÜNSTLERLEBEN"

A warm June night in a little Minnesota town; a few neighbors leave their indoor electric amusements for a while to smell the soft air, to watch the cut grass darken in the long sundown. Across the street, a ramshackle house flanked by rusty cars.

It's the new Mexicans in town, maybe twenty of them, all outside on the front lawn. Too many of them for that little house, but you know how they breed. Just look at that piebald paint, the crumbled stoop, the thriving thistles.

They're not like us—all that black hair, those brown legs in shorts, the smell of chilies fried in lard, the sound of trilled Rs, low laughter on a foreign tongue. Not like us, the neighbors nod.

Soon there's music loud enough for us to hear, clear across the street. What *are* they doing? They're dancing—waltzing—the whole lot of them to Johann Strauss, "Künstlerleben." Old ladies with boys, women with women, men with little girls, probably some new combination of lovers. Where do they think they are? Vienna in 1889? Not like us.

Soon they all join hands in a chain to circle the unkempt lawn in their pointy boots, sandals, brown bare feet. The waltz goes on and on with all the repeats, then over again. The light above the ash trees turns lavender and burnt orange. One, two, three.

The neighbors cluck: *what* do they think they are doing? Just look at that. Waltzing. On a summer night. To the "Artist's Life." Not like us.

GIRL EATING RICE — WUHAN 1992

Dinner on a dusty February night in a teacher's cramped cement flat.
After cooking, she comes in to eat leftovers, carrying a bowl of rice.
Rice steam curls up around her black hair. Her face is like an ancient
Chinese painting trying to explain to the future what it meant to be
beautiful in an old, long-gone dynasty. That could be a pipa in her
hands instead of a bowl of rice; her black chopsticks could be plectra.
She plays the rice as much as eats it, each mouthful perfect as an old
poem, sung slowly, a little tinkling laughter and a wrinkling of the eyes
between bites, like sighs of pleasure at how the tune goes.

I sit there, neither listening to nor understanding the hum of Chinese
talk around the table. I can't keep my eyes either off her rice or her
opera hands moving from bowl to lips to a cold morsel of pepper or
pork.

She is not an old painting of music at all but a lovely young girl in a
lavender sweater who has cooked a long time for her husband's old
teacher. Yet she is the other, too, thousands of years old, a girl from the
mountains of such beauty and grace that the emperor sees her eating
rice in the palace kitchen and weeps for his passing life and the misery
of his country.

MUSICAL SHOPPING IN WUCHANG — 1992

"Jambalaya" blasts over and over from the tape shop speakers in front
of Zhong Nan department store. Big fun on the bayou as thousands
of Old Hundred Names, escaping their cold cramped flats, stream by
to admire the new goods: a purple bicycle, a plastic food chopper, an
automatic rice pot, a mushroom lamp, a blond Barbie, a boom box
from Japan. Son of a gun! If we keep quiet, we could own this or that!
Two old ladies emerge into daylight cradling magnums of Chinese
champagne to celebrate the filé gumbo.

Out in the street, the hawkers all sell double-sided plastic photo cards of
Mao with two red tassels hanging down. On one face, the solemn old
wart who scowls out from the Gate of Heavenly Peace; on the other,
the young romantic pink—cheeked wart in worker's cap. Hang him
in the wind and see how he ages! In taxi, office window, restaurant
door, the old boy blows round and round, bringing good luck and
safe trips, tassels swinging to the happy jambalaya beat coming from
everywhere but inside.

CAPITALIST MUSIC ON LUOSHI ROAD — WUHAN 1992

At the Sunday street market, three shabby men, the Music Torture Orchestra, move from peddler to peddler. The erhu player scratches out a tune that sounds like Grand Old Opry. The young one sings in a harsh falsetto clacking his two loud sticks to keep time. The wizened old man on a crutch holds out his palm till money crosses it.

At the feel of a few jiao, the music stops in midstroke. Crutch hops to the next peddler with newly empty palm, and the tune resumes until more jiao appear. The peddlers pay up grudgingly so that real customers can come spend. The music protection racket moves on.

A hundred peddlers at their Sunday stalls in earshot. Sometimes the trio gets out only a few scratchy bars, only a few stick clacks, before the bought silence. Sometimes a stubborn peddler makes them finish a whole verse. Maybe he likes this free market music better than haggling over cabbages or reed brooms.

This backward jukebox disappears down the street, *diminuendo poco a poco,* crutch hopping from stall to stall like a human metronome.

ART TATUM

1949, a club on 52nd Street, Manhattan, midnight, the century almost half gone, two wars under its belt, America half tight with victory and easy money. A big pear-shaped black man in pale suit, buttoned vest, jaunty silk pocket handkerchief, polka-dot tie a little loose, walks through the backstage door, touches the black wing of the piano, feels his way down its curve to the bench. The waiter brings him a mug of beer, sets it on a coaster at the end of the keyboard. The pear-shaped man nods, turns his head to the customers, shows them his clouded irises, smiles the awkward smile of a man who has never rehearsed his own face in a mirror, then finds the keyboard with his hands. The bar is dark, smoky, clouds of Pall-Malls, Kools, Chesterfields, girls in short skirts and lacy stockings bringing loaded trays of Manhattans, Old-Fashioneds, Seven-Sevens, Boilermakers, lipstick-blotted napkins, whiff of Bay Rum and Emeraude, the click of a Zippo, a few seconds of muffled laughter, the silvery ring of a quarter tip dropped to the floor.

He starts to play, just a note or two rocking back and forth in the middle of the piano like a first lesson; he smiles down at the keyboard, his friend, his servant. Then the piano jumps, wobbles, erupts in a glitter of scales, arpeggios, fioriture, chords barging into each other, as if astonished with themselves for sounding together in such a sequence, "Tea for Two," here a bar of Mozart, there ragtime, here a hymn, there a tango, everything stewed together with surprise and speed, now two hands, now three, now four, now eight, as if the pear body sprouted into a calm octopus squeezing music out of the ivories with his pudgy tentacles.

He hardly pauses between the slabs of music; the tune makes no difference: "Begin the Beguine," "Heart and Soul," "Honey-Suckle Rose," "The Tiger Rag," "Willow, Weep for Me," "To a Wild Rose," snatches of Grieg, Gershwin, "The Kerry Dance," Bach. This is the naked face of music itself, eighty-eight keys plugged straight into the nervous system, inanimate piano transmogrified into pear-shaped body.

Around the dark bar, a little applause starts: there's John Bull in the corner with his ruffed collar and black hat, fresh from the Globe Theatre; there's Domenico Scarlatti, wig askew, slapping the table with his palms while his mammoth belly jiggles; there's Franz Liszt in his black soutane jotting down fingerings on a napkin, muttering "Mon Dieu!," knocking back his cognac; there's Scott Joplin, looking solemn as a preacher, whispering "Slow down a little, Art! Not so many notes!"; there's nerdy Glenn Gould, only seventeen and too young to drink, watching the pedal go almost untouched, noting the squeaky clean counterpoint.

These are the customers the pear-shaped man with the dapper handkerchief always wanted when he sat down at a piano, saw with his dim eyes the brilliant light flickering inside the ivory, and shape-shifted into music itself.

GLENN GOULD 1932–1982

A man who played the piano with as much genius as it is possible to contain in a human being said he trusted machines and electricity more than he trusted humans in a room. Henceforth, he would play only for steel wire and thin tape, genius saved from coughing, wheezing and all possibility of disagreeable whispers and remarks.

He took his first machine, the piano, and chiseled, filed, and muffled it until it suited his music and was like no other such machine on earth—a name brand of one. He sat on his second machine, an old chair that squeaked and rocked and comforted him.

He waited until the middle of the night to have perfect silence for his music, then moved his two peculiar machines into a sealed sound-locked room where not even the vibration of a human foot could ever be felt. There he played, safe at last from the rest of us, and even, he thought, from himself.

But when Bach or Haydn came on him, he started singing in a low and ugly hum, out of tune with everything his hands were doing. No machine could take this noise away or clear it out without losing the music, too, so he was left with an awful choice. Give up principle or give up beauty.

He chose the music, hums and all, a glad hypocrite like us. Only failed ideals and wrong turnings will ever get you anywhere on earth or make anything with beauty or energy inside it. In the Bach F♯ Minor Fugue, or the slow C major tune in the Haydn sonata, the awful humming overwhelms the perfect technology and everyone with ears tuned right is glad of it.

That hum is his ghost, still alive, but also it is the invisible audience sneezing and hacking; it is the ignorant applause after the wrong movement; it is pigeons in the rafters of the hall, cooing for bread; it is me blowing my nose and wiping my tears of joy in this music—in this odd, grand failure of a man.

J. S. BACH: F♯ MINOR TOCCATA

This music weeps, not for sin
but rather for the black fact
that we must all die, but not one
of us knows what comes after.
This music leaps from key to key
as if it had no clear place to arrive,
making up its life, one bar at a time.
But when you come at last to the real theme,
strict, inexorable, and bleak,
you must play it slow and sad,
with melancholy dignity, or you miss
all its grim wisdom.
In three pages, it says, the universe collapses,
and you—still only halfway home.

PRACTICING THE BLUMENFELD ETUDE FOR THE LEFT HAND ALONE

Forget, after a while, the right hand exists at all.
Whatever it's up to is no concern of yours,
whether pulling a trigger, counting change,
unfastening a dress. Maybe it's even
practicing yet another etude
for some silent interior piano. Meanwhile
your single sinister hand plays over and over
a stretch of notes, till even the fourth finger obeys,
wrist rotating on the pivot of the magisterial thumb,
an airplane doing show tricks in midair
banking this way and that to dazzle the crowd.
Such music your five fingers make!
The right hand is jealous now, an ignored
lover waiting for the phone to ring.

III

FREE MARKET WIND

MY OLD FRIEND AT&T WRITES ME A PERSONAL LETTER

"Dear Mr. Holm,
Post office box one-eighty-seven may
be a terrific place to live, but for you—
it's more than just a home.
It's also a place to do serious business. . . ."
Dear Company,
How well you understand
my needs—my life—
how every night we light
tiny candles to dine
on a roast sparrow (nowhere
for leftovers, you know),
drink a small young burgundy
(no space here for wine to grow
old and big), then lie down
on our narrow bed for a little love.
Early in the morning
third class mail tumbles
down the chute to drive us out
into the street. We only do
serious business here
when blizzards far away
stop the mail trucks or the master
takes a three-day holiday.

It would be nice to move.
Our place is a little cramped,
but we think your offer of
a "telecommunications program
designed exclusively to meet
the needs of people like me"
will make life better.
Please send more details
in a registered letter.
Maybe we should talk face-
to-face: our box or yours?
I notice you, like us,
live in a box, ten seventy-eight
in Duncansville, PA.
That's why you understand.
Sincerely, your old friend,
Mr. Holm.

AMERICAN NEWS

Six o'clock on a gray February morning.
The radio alarm snaps to attention.
The news murmurs of blow jobs,
tobacco plots, semen-stained dresses,
a fetus in formaldehyde.
Another morning in America.
Then nine words arrive calmly
as if they were the weather report:
"An attack on Iraq could trigger
a market rally." *Leaves of Grass*
leaps off the shelf, the pages
burst into flame, fanning each other
as they blacken to ash. The notes fall
from the scores of Charles Ives, gather
up into a pile of bug corpses at
the foot of the piano. Louis Sullivan's
Owatonna bank collapses into
its own center as if hit with
a smart bomb. Now Dow Jones
snarls under its wolf-hide cloak.
The NASDAQ index bares its teeth.
This news comes just in time
to get us ready for one more good
day at the office, one more meeting
at which dollar bills shower down
over the table like pale green rice.

CORPORATE WIND

The Company pays hard cash for all the wind
blowing over these bare hills near Dakota,
Chinook, Alberta Clipper, Tornado,
then raises up a thousand bone-white poles
topped with three blades to slice the air,
transform it into kilowatts of power.
Daily this must astonish the cows
who still graze on private grass below.
The Company says it owns this wind
in perpetuity or at least until
the glacier comes to collect the hills again.
In bright fall sun the blades all circle,
each in its own time, this way and that,
free market wind still dancing its own dance.

HALLELUJAH AT THE SIOUX FALLS AIRPORT

At the bar at the Joe Foss Field
in Sioux Falls, South Dakota,
a few idlers sipping whiskey
wait for late airplanes to arrive.
Not a soul says a word,
but out of the silence comes nasal music,
a familiar tune: "Hallelujah!
Hallelujah, The Lord God
Omnipotent Reigneth,"
sings the video poker machine.
Maybe somebody filled an inside straight,
always cause for praise and rejoicing.
For applause, quarters clatter
down the metal birth canal.
Silence again at Joe Foss Field.
Not a soul looks up from his whiskey
or sings a loud Amen, or toasts
the omnipotence of luck.

WITHOUT TV

Suddenly you are gone from the United States without ever going anywhere. A tree branch scratches across the glass; daylight evaporates out the west window; someone lights the lamp; the icebox clicks on and hums; two humans come and say something, a rhythm of silence and thought. After a little while the guests look uneasy, ask: Where is it?

One day it fell into the old cistern. Though we listened for a long time, we haven't heard it hit bottom: Maybe it's still falling.

But what do you do all day without games, laughter, good news, specials?

We listen for the owl who sometimes perches all night in the silver maple, hooting and hunting; sometimes we hear his wings whooshing down on a rabbit, a snake, maybe a cat. When the owl goes elsewhere, we hear a violin missing notes a block or two away. We hear pages turn.

But aren't you lonely, bored?

Not since it started falling; maybe when it hits bottom, a little shiver of regret will ruffle the curtains a bit, but then we'll go to a store and buy something in its honor.

MRI

What is the pain like? says the pretty girl with the clipboard.
Like a serrated bread knife sawing at the top of the rib cage,
    punctuated with sudden blows from an ax or a meat cleaver.
What she wanted was "not too bad" or "pretty bad," or even "bad," an
    anonymous quality, sans detail, sans metaphor.
A little stoicism might have cheered her up.
Are you claustrophobic? she asks, with another nod at the clipboard.
Of course, I answer. Isn't everyone, if they are still alive?
Can I give you something for it?
Only the lead gift in the twilight if that's what it comes to.
What?
Never mind.
How do you feel, she asks, after she has slid my supine body into the
    tight white sarcophagus.
Like a character in a Poe story.
No, I work for Dr. Moe.
Not much lit. in the med-tech course, I suppose.
Lots of people like music, she nods cheerfully.
What have you got?
Easy listening, soft rock, country . . .
No Mahler Ninth? No C# minor quartet?
Give me the news, I say. Ashcroft and the collapsing stock market seem
    about right.
It's noisy, she warns.
She has the gift for understatement.

It is like being squeezed into an airless plastic coffin dropped on the
    floor of a sheet metal factory stamping out auto parts or shell
    casings. Irregular metallic thumping and whanging.
Only an hour left, she says after ten years.
Just lay real still. We're getting good pictures.
Not since the Middle Ages has anyone thought of a machine like this,
a modern rack or iron maiden to take pictures of the spine, the organs,
    the bones, the muscles.
Torquemada would have used it to take pictures of your opinions.
He would have offered his heretics prayer but neither easy listening
    nor Valium.
He thought this God's will. We think it science.
This is, I suppose, progress of a kind.
One way or another, you wind up diagnosed.
Either that or burned at the stake, another kind of diagnosis.

DELOS IN THE RAIN
OCTOBER 30, 2000

for Wynn Binger and Dick and Susan Lundell

I

Thirty yellow-jacketed American cruisers
tour Delos alone on a rumbly dark morning
in almost November. The island is theirs
if they want to sack and pillage,
joining the long throng of three thousand years
of Delos' sackers and pillagers.
All night they sailed west from the Turkish coast,
their small ship thrashed by gales,
barrels of rain, timpanis of thunder,
a riled black sea slashed by lightning,
but they tell each other politely, cheerfully
that they slept well, the sea meant no harm.
They are, after all, Midwesterners entering their fourth score
with a little money, a few diseases, the odd catastrophe,
but, as their parents taught them to say with a shrug:
"Not too bad. Could be worse. We're pretty good."

II

They land at Delos off the old ferry under a heavy sky.
The light drizzle troubles them less

than smelly Greek boat toilets.
Now they stand on the stony island
where Apollo and Artemis were born of the goddess
who clutched the single palm in sight to squeeze them out.
The tree—maybe the very one—still stands alone
in a dry lake bed girdled by scrub brush.
But barring that, nothing grows here—
only gardens of broken marble, gravel, rubble.
Delos looks a place where no rain fell
since stones heaved up from under the earth.
The guidebook warns of lizards, adders,
but in almost November, they all sleep.

III

Pentilos—the group guide—summons the yellow jackets.
He spreads his arms, wiggles his fingers, catches their eye—
begins reciting the long history of this barren place
so like the whole history of the human race—
temples of gold, treasuries guarded by gods,
profits from the slave trade,
tons of marble ferried in from the empire,
thirty-ton slabs, pink, blue, gray, white,
heaved off ships by a hundred shoulders,
marble all the way up the mountain,
columns, statues, pilasters, urns, frescoes,
built, broken, built and broken again
by Athens, Naxos, Egypt, Pontos,

Rome, Athens again, Sparta, Macedonia,
always more blood, a litter of corpses,
the gold gone on a fast ship.

IV

Today the rain pelts down over Delos
and Pentilos and thirty yellow jackets,
two millennia of overdue rain, not
an unbroken roof in sight to hide from it.
Pentilos leads the yellow jackets
to the frescoes in Dionysius' house,
then to the ruined amphitheater,
where he acts the birth of drama,
single-handed, playing all parts
as rain leaks off his balding head, his waving fingers.

V

The miracle in Delos in almost November
in this garden of marble rubble
once the Hong Kong and Vatican of the world,
now poor, bare, ruined, but above all, wet,
is rain that keeps slithering down into the socks
of thirty aging yellow-jacket cruisers
come halfway around the world
to see what the United States might look like in a while,
what three-score of their own used life
looks like to their children, who will find out

for themselves, that even the whitest marble,
the bravest army, the richest gods
protect you neither from lizards nor adders, nor sackers,
nor rain. Still, they think, by tonight,
we will all be in a warm boat with dry socks,
and they are right. The yellow jackets lived through
a little rain, a little history,
and will live through a little more.

LOOKING AT GOD

for Bill "Cutz" Klas

"Drive eight miles west on Stampede Road. It's good gravel; when it dead-ends, you should see the mountain if it's out," say the locals.

"How will I know it?"

"If it's there, you'll know it."

I drive eight miles, past the In-His-Shadows Church, a wrecked pickup with a peace symbol dangling from a bent rearview mirror, a half dozen cabins, up past heavy woods to high tundra, still snowless at the end of October, brown hummocks, red weeds, punctuated with an occasional mealy spruce. Eight-Mile Lake is half-frozen, dark blue polka-dotted with ice.

At the end of the road, there it is—two peaks, immense white shadows poking above the other ridges, bigger than anything ought to be at eighty miles distance. The locals are right: if you can't tell you are in the presence of God when you see it, no one can explain it to you.

I remember an old friend in Minnesota who calls Lake Superior God, because it is always there—even when it is invisible, and you can't see across it when it isn't. Another might call the Grand Canyon God. They're all right. The point is: God is big—too big to miss, no matter

how the human race wants to shrivel him down to size and buddy up.
If you let God into your heart he will explode it like a toy balloon.

God is the heart—of the spacious firmament of all the circling galaxies.

I turn off the pickup, and stand transfixed—listening. No wind,
no motors, no birds, no talk, bright sun, maybe thirty degrees. The
pickup pistons ping a little as they lose heat, then they fall silent too.
It is the loudest silence I have ever heard, and it goes on for miles. Is
this silence the noise of the mountain singing anthems to itself? Is it
the noise of the joints inside the axis of the planet, rotating? Is the air
praying? A half-hour of this is enough—too much. I start the pickup
and return downhill, every way you can go.

DENALI, ALASKA

THE PARANOIA OF HAPPY SKEPTICS
VISITING THE WEST COAST

Driving north out of California, I imagine that I have escaped
religion. No more Tibetan Buddhists, Zen meditators, Krishna
monks, spiritual vegetarians, and holistic self-actualizers. Somewhere
around Sausalito, there is a small factory which stamps out religions
like precision machine parts. Are the screws stripped on your old
beliefs? Have your spiritual gears started slipping? On each full moon
night next to the Pacific, the truth truck rumbles out to make home
deliveries, C.O.D. . . . an illustrated Koran for Peterson, the essence of
the Bhagavad Gita for Bloomberg, a retooled Zoroaster for Martinelli,
"How I changed my diet and found God" for Lopez. But surely not
in Washington, I think, as I cross the border north from Oregon on
the freeway, not here in this rainy Norwegian north, where even the
pine trees look like agnostics growing by the millions next to the
concrete road, silent to each other, silent about God, silent about
the afterlife in a book, or a table, or as plywood siding. I stop for gas
north of Kelso, the air heavy with the damp sour smell of a pulp
mill. I browse while the tank fills, notice Christian pamphlets piled
up between the grease guns and tire gauges. I head out fast and stop
in the first motel. It is now pouring rain. The only magazine on the
bedside table is the *Christian Athlete*. The television is tuned to the
Evangelists. I get nervous and light a cigarette . . . no ashtray. The
Gideon Bible is lying open to Corinthians on the coffee table; a small
ashtray is hidden in the drawer. The typed notice back of the door tells
me to get out by 11:00 A.M., also that while stealing the towel might

not *seem* wrong, God hates a thief, and we, the management, intend to do His will by prosecuting you—for your own spiritual good. I get an uneasy night's sleep and stop for breakfast at the first coffee shop north. An aggressively smiley waitress seats me next to the book rack: "The Christian Family Library." I pick one up: . . . stories of the happy handicapped. "How I became a triple amputee and found Jesus." I put it back fast, as if it were made of burning sulfur, and reach for a napkin. I get a pamphlet instead, lodged between the salt and pepper; in addition to wishing me a really nice day, it wants to know if I am all right with Jesus. I leave the eggs, run to the car, lurch back onto the freeway and speed away. The Mozart quartet on public radio fades out behind the first curve and Gospel Rock blares at me, uninvited, unwelcome, unwholesome, unsavory. "I want to know more about Jesus," unleaded Jesus, self-serve Jesus, Jesus between the sheets, magic-fingers Jesus, Jesus provided for your sanitary comfort, climate-control Jesus, Egg McJesus, Jesus over-easy, whole-wheat Jesus, pecan Jesus, decaf Jesus, refried Jesus, rock-a-bye Jesus . . . SWEET JESUS! One sight of the Pacific Ocean and God by whatever name he arrives, Jesus or Jones or the Ace of Spades, clutches you hard by the heart; now you must have truth, by God, absolute, unforgiving, sterling silver, poured concrete truth like a stone bracelet to weigh down your arm as it watches over all this rolling water washing toward Asia and the light.

OFFICIAL TALK IN WUHAN — 1992

When nothing has happened there is no need
to mention it, it would only prove
embarrassing if certain policies
were brought up, though of course
everything, as you see, is fully
ordinary, moving forward, though without
any backward to move forward
from and everyone smiles and is
happy, doing their part, though of what
they are not too sure, only little
months and years have disappeared,
nothing much and nothing serious if
a little time goes quietly away
here and there, and isn't mentioned because
there's no need, really, besides what
good would it do anyone, it might
cause painful thoughts and you can
see for yourself clearly the shops
are full, there's plenty to eat, the future's
just around the corner, and the past
is looking better every day. Meanwhile
an old lizard the size of a bulldozer
perches on the flat cement roof.
All the sleepers in their cold flats
listen to his raspy breathing all night,

watch his scaly tail hang just over
the edge, wave back and forth past their window,
thud into the wall now and then
like a hanged body blown
against the gallows by the east wind.

AN EARLY MORNING CAFÉ

I

One hundred and seven stories into the air
the Windows on the World Café
served pâté and poached salmon
to diners staring over Manhattan,
but early this September morning,
the sommelier and mâitre d'
were still asleep in their faraway flats,
only the sous-chef and banquet staff
had arrived to peel the shrimp,
trim the artichokes and wash
the leaves of the escarole.

II

Simple work with your mates
in a quiet early morning café
is a pleasure: jokes, mild complaining,
a hummed tune or two,
when suddenly a berserk machine
decides to murder a building with fire.
Like a badly shot elephant,
the hundred-and-six stories holding up
your peeling knife and lettuce drier
wobbled and shook a little while,

but when flames melted the bones
it all tumbled down on top of itself
in a gray heap, shrimp,
artichokes, escarole, fifty thousand
bottles of elegant wine,
and you yourself, unless you leapt
out one of the windows of the world
to finish with imaginary wings
the flight to the city of angels.

III

Humans so riddled with hate they turned
from men to bombs smashed the girders
under your café, though they'd never met you,
to murder you for the glory of God
with your apron still smeared with shrimp guts.
It was always thus. Try to kill an abstraction
by murdering a building from the air,
but all you kill is Bob and Edna
and Sollie and Rodrigo and Mei-Mei.
A building is only a set of artificial legs
to hold up human beings in the air,
and an airplane only a sheet of folded paper.
But fifty thousand bottles of good wine
and a hundred pounds of fresh Gulf shrimp,
and Bob and Edna and all the rest—
that is something real!

IV

If you think you've bagged the one truth
and that truth wants final sacrifice,
then you've stepped outside the human race,
and your plane will not land in heaven
wherever you think it might be.
Heaven is an early morning café
wherever you are.

PAUL WELLSTONE — OCTOBER 25, 2002

On a gray sleety October day
the plane goes down in the north woods
with the large-hearted senator
whose decency and respect for old ideals
made half the citizens almost happy
to be Americans in a dark time.
Down went his wife and his daughter too,
three campaign workers, two pilots,
eight in all, the radio says,
neglecting the ninth seat where Death
dressed in an ordinary suit
sat watching for his chance
to do a morning's harvesting.
Do you think he wasn't there
hitching a ride, invisible, just as
he sat in the box at Ford's Theatre,
held open the convertible door in Dallas?
He sits in the front seat of your car, too,
or waits feigning sleep with his head
resting on the next pillow in your bed.
So we go on to write the same poem,
sing the same sad song yet once more
not for the dead who have gone
over to the insensible kingdom
but for us who must now carry on

without them. This time, as so often
before, Death snatched a big one
when we could not stand to lose
his voice that spoke, not alone,
but for us millions who longed
for a world green, alive, about to bloom.

THE SEA EATS WHAT IT PLEASES

If you turn your back to the ocean
Do you think the tide will not find you
If it decides to rise a little higher
Than usual, to swallow an extra helping
Of gravel, to suck on your bones to clean
Its palate? The sea eats what it pleases
Whether you face it or give it your back.
No use having opinions about this.
But the sea does not hate you, or imagine
That you have wounded it with your avarice.
You cannot blaspheme the honor of water
Or insult the tide for tasting of salt.
Only humans, so newly risen from fish,
Imagine drowning each other for reasons.

IV

THE WORLD IS ENOUGH

WATER TANGO IN THE SEA OF CORTEZ

for Julia and Marcy

Two women, one short, one tall,
stand in the sand to face the waves
as if the sea were their lover come
twice a day to tickle them.
They like this!, play coquette,
waiting for a swollen breaker
to soak them with spray, feigning
surprise, then dancing away just
slow enough for foam to lick their toes.
The men who've lost interest in
dancing the tango with the surf
stand above the oncoming tide
to admire these women playing sea nymph.
They are jealous of the water.
One quotes Walt: "Dash me with amorous wet,"
while the women, disdaining literature,
continue being dashed, and liking it,
repaying the crooked fingers of the sea.

ECOLOGICAL ANOREXIA OUTSIDE TUCSON

Earth's been
on a diet
too long
around here,
a starved woman
never quite
lovely as
she thinks.
Bones stick through.
Hair fell off.
Wind blew
eyes out of
the cliff.
Not much here
soft enough
even to feed
a buzzard.
Cactus knuckles,
gravel stew,
a kitchen full
of lizards who
disapprove
of you—

fat
guest
in
a thin
house.

SILENCE IN NORTH DAKOTA

On the lip of the Killdeer Canyon
five hundred feet over the tan buttes
that flank the little Missouri
in the middle of North Dakota
in the middle of North America
in the middle of the western hemisphere
on tax day in the middle of April
at almost the end of the second millennium
the universe held its breath
for a full minute.

Complete, inviolate silence—
not a crow cawed
not a frog croaked
the wind shut its mouth
the cars and tractors stopped
the TVs all went dead
words failed for no good reason
clouds scudded but kept quiet about it
and everything alive or
what is sometimes called not-alive
listened to everything else
stones, motors, crocuses, blood pulsing

And then the crow cawed,
(that seemed to be the signal)
and the universe exhaled
and everything started again
but for that minute we heard
what it was really like.

THISTLES

Always the kid's job to kill thistles.
Strap on your tin tank of 2-4-D.
Raise up your sprayer with its plastic hose,
The umbilical cord for the poison.
They stand there, arrogantly alive
In the wheat, flax, oats, beans, alfalfa:
Golden-flowered sow thistle,
Purple horny Canadians,
Bull thistle, pig weed, buffalo burr, cocklebur.
Dowse them with death mist.
At first they feel nothing,
No trembling in the armored stalk,
But come back tomorrow—
Dried heads slumped to one side,
Green leaching toward corpse gray.
In a week, they'll be finished.
Does the wheat smile? Does the alfalfa sigh?
Does the flax nod as if it wished
To pat you on the head and say:
Good boy. Job well done.
That's farm work for children.
Behead the chickens, castrate the pigs,
Poison the thistles. Teach them

What the world is going to be like.
Don't weep too hard for the thistles.
They will be back next year.
They will outlast you. Always.
That's what you learn from them.

COELACANTH

In February, in tropical summer, we tour the marine museum in
Tulear, west coast of Madagascar. It's a humid hundred inside and
out. Even the bottles of formaldehyde sweat. Specimen after vinegary
specimen of strange fish: "Endemique!" "Unique!" "Extinct!" Finally,
the back room—what everyone comes to see after enduring the two
hundred bottles of briny spines. The soft-spoken gold-skinned girl
flips the fluorescent light, points—the pièce de résistance of fishdom:
Coelacanth caught in the Mozambique Channel, the fish that should
have been dead for seventy-five million years, that never evolved, that
lives only in this hot and lonesome ocean east of Africa.

He floats in a long glass tank, facing us. Five feet of mud flaps, a shit-
brown, bug-eyed lump, stumpy double fins, underslung jaw, spiny mess
of a rudder. Was the carpenter of this Platonic form of ugliness drunk,
dim-witted, asleep at the helm of the ship of creation? This . . . this . . .
this . . . How did this breathe . . . swim . . . survive . . . ? Was this too
ugly even for the million sleek and ravenous Indian Ocean sharks to
eat? Yet live it did, and does at this very moment, in the gray waters
west of this room, this Quasimodo fish, this Phantom of Ichthyology,
this ghost comrade of the pterodactyl.

Does Coelacanth broadcast news of what you looked like before you
started your slow crawl out of the water, dropping your gills and your
swim bladder in the tidal mud to stand upright in the sun, flexing your
arrogant opposable thumbs?

Bend down now. Press your lips to the tank. Kiss the Coelacanth, offering praise and thanks that he became the fish of sorrows, the one who stayed behind to atone for your sins in his flesh. Whatever swims in the Indian Ocean swims inside you, too, the antique useless parts, the old ugliness, the unevolved vitality that says: Stay alive! Stay alive! Stay alive!

A VISIT WITH FRED MANFRED'S GHOST —
BLUE MOUNDS, 1997

In this house cut into the red bluff
a tall man sat in a low room
scribbling book after book after book.
When paper wearied of him, he rose up
from his chair and strolled to the hilltop.

On a July afternoon, pink wild roses,
yellow prickly pears, all in bloom,
cool north wind stirring up the grass,
he stood on some red rock outcrop
surveying three states stretched out below
and thought this world a suitable home
for a tall man scribbling in a low room.

On another fine July afternoon
three years after neighbors claim he died,
I stroll up to admire the cactus blooming
but find him still there, standing on red quartz
reciting a page or two of the big new book
that will finally open their eyes in New York.

His voice sounds like north wind through grass.
His gnarly finger, twice too long, points downhill
at a world that still looks suitable
for a tall man scribbling in a low room,
catching rides home on a slow billow of cloud.

JOHN CLARE'S LAST LETTER

Browsing one day in the college library, I find on the shelf the letters
of mad John Clare, a gay pink book. I wonder what old Clare said
in his last letter after all those years in the loony bin? He wrote on
March 8, 1860 to James Hipkins, an "unknown inquirer from the
outside world." Clare was sixty-seven years old, twenty-three years
locked up, four to go until the end. The editor says in his neat brackets,
"This letter was [sent]." Most asylum letters never made it to the post.
The letter says:

> Dear sir:
> I am in a Madhouse and quite forget
> your name or who you are you must excuse
> me for I have nothing to communicate or
> tell of and why I am shut up I don't know I
> have nothing to say so I conclude.
> Yours respectfully,
> John Clare

Who was Hipkins? Why did he write? Had he fallen in love with
those poems full of wrens, mice, badgers, larks, flies, crows, fish, snipes,
owls, moles, and imaginary wives? Did he weep when Clare's little
note came back to him in the "outside" world?

I leaf through the other last madhouse letters. Clare wrote to a son, long dead, inquiring if the boy ever saw his sister, even longer dead. Had life and death ceased to make any difference to him? Was that his madness—that he couldn't tell the difference between one world and the next, between the quick and the dead? Had the walls between worlds fallen down inside him, so that angels, devils, ghosts, specters, moved calmly back and forth between them?

The gay pink book falls open to the flyleaf. There's a name—Alec Bond—in neat red pen—long dead Alec who loved mad John Clare and gay pink books and owls and badgers and even his old friend, me!

Those walls fall down inside me too, and I catch myself asking questions that will have to wait a long time to be answered. Sometimes I think I'm shut up, too, and can't tell why and ought, respectfully, to conclude.

But sometimes, in empty libraries on muggy September days in Minnesota, the letters arrive with my name, written in a language I can read. News passes jauntily between worlds.

When this happens, what need does a man have to make anything up? The world is enough if you can say plainly what happens. If you say it plain enough, like mad John Clare, sometimes they shut you up, though what difference that makes no one can yet tell.

WEDDING POEM

*for Kristofer Dignus and Maria Heba, August 2000, Vík í Myrdal,
and for Schele and Phil, July 2002, Minneapolis*

A marriage is risky business these days
Says some old and prudent voice inside.
We don't need twenty children anymore
To keep the family line alive,
Or gather up the hay before the rain.
No law demands respectability.
Love can arrive without certificate or cash.
History and experience both make clear
That men and women do not hear
The music of the world in the same key,
Rather rolling dissonances doomed to clash.

So what is left to justify a marriage?
Maybe only the hunch that half the world
Will ever be present in any room
With just a single pair of eyes to see it.
Whatever is invisible to one
Is to the other an enormous golden lion
Calm and sleeping in the easy chair.
After many years, if things go right
Both lion and emptiness are always there;
The one never true without the other.

But the dark secret of the ones long married,
A pleasure never mentioned to the young,
Is the sweet heat made from two bodies in a bed
Curled together on a winter night,
The smell of the other always in the quilt,
The hand set quietly on the other's flank
That carries news from another world
Light-years away from the one inside
That you always thought you inhabited alone.
The heat in that hand could melt a stone.

V

ABOUT THIS ONE LAST WISH

———

FOR DR. MIKE DOMAN, 1945–1991

A NOTE ON THE DOOR

One night I arrive at the door,
find a note: "I am sick.
Come in quietly." I don't need
to be told. The handwriting
gave me the news. While he aged
a month, it aged a century.

Now that hand wobbles
as if it walked the page
on a three-pronged cane
that can't find a safe spot
on the ice-covered index card.

I ask another doctor why
the hand gets news of death
long before the head. He
doesn't know, but knows
it's true. If the handwriting
firms up again, the patient
might live. If not . . .

Write a note on the margin
of this page. Look for signs:
a leaning *t,* a woozy *s,*
an *i* with curvature of the spine.

THE SANITY OF DENIAL

I

"Where we're going, there'll be wind, plenty of wind.
Best be prepared for anything." He says this
standing in his bathtub, held up by four arms;
weak legs wasted almost to bone wobble under him.
Two friends washed him to bring his fever down,
squeezing lukewarm water over what little meat
still sticks to his skeleton after fevers ate
their fill of liver, marrow, eyes, brain.
In the tub, he absently twirls his opal ring
twice too big for its finger, after these months
while exotic diseases washed over him,
tidal waves crashing into his body
one after another without relent: As soon as one
surge subsides, held back by passion and will,
another, more massive, smashes in. Under it all,
the black swell at the seawall
loosened every foundation stone.

His bones told him the monkey virus
had tucked its napkin in and settled down
to eat long before his doctor's brain
that still kept faith with science and reason.

2

At the sea in Oregon we retreated
for a winter to listen to windblown tide
thump onto the rocks. In March,
the sky warmed, the sun beat back
the stubborn Pacific clouds, and three of us
climbed a little hill to an old lighthouse.
The warm grass astonished us, the new
yellow wildflowers tickled our bare feet.
We lay high above the noisy sea for hours,
the mammoth Victorian glass eye in the tower
turning and turning slowly above us.

We talked a little, praising the day, good luck,
good company, the sweetness of the world,
mostly silent as the sea winds
crawled slowly up the cliffs
to riffle the grass and cool our supine bodies.
To breathe, see, touch, listen, smell
on such an afternoon is enough.

Children arrived with noise, talk pilfered
from television, so we trudged back to the car.

What is there not to deny if this sweet world
were abruptly eaten out from under your own body

leaving it falling into a black hole?
Who, in his right mind, would not say No!
shouting it into the gathering wind
with all the power left inside him?

LIVING WILL / WILL TO LIVE

He wants to die in his own house,
on his own couch, looking out
at the gray lake, the red flowers,
the big white volcano.
In America this takes money.
The poor go to anonymous beds.
No one is sure who is still
at home in his head, so the robust-
voiced doctor holds his hand, saying
"Are you with us? Are you there?"
It is only days from the end,
and we all know it. He nods
weakly, pulling at his dried lips.

Ten of us circle the couch,
legal witnesses, loving courtiers.
The gleaming oak floor, black piano,
lid closed like a coffin,
soft light from the lake
flooding in through the window—
a tree of red poinsettias,
tan cat asleep on a table.
It will be Christmas soon.

This is a theater now, the house
motionless, waiting, the gray
dying man at center stage.
Silence. More silence. More.
Twenty eyes on the dry lip.
"I want to live." More silence.
"Do you want to go to the hospital?"
Still more silence. "No."
The doctor reads a legal paper
stating that he has agreed to die.
It's this or procedures. "Yes."

The State is satisfied.
But he still wants to live —
to rise from the couch, shower,
take everyone to dinner,
look wryly over his glasses
as bowls of cold crab arrive,
say, "The black dog of hunger
beaten safely from the door again,"
to come home to this big window,
drink brandy in thin snifters,
talk a little of politics or plays,
watch boat lights snake across the lake
five hundred feet below his red flowers.

He will write each disease a check,
send it from the door.

But twenty eyes, the robust doctor
still holding his gray bony hand,
know there will be no walking
from this room, the world
shrunk to piano, tree, cat, couch,
objects themselves moving closer
to him, until soon they will become
invisible, back of the eye, dark.

Still he wants to live,
and about this one last wish,
nothing can be done.

PLAYING THE BLACK PIANO

One day when his eyes flicker with a little life, I go to the big black
Yamaha across from his hospital bed, the piano he bought for friends
and old age, but after the test, started practicing himself—slowly,
methodically, badly, mathematical fingers playing like a doctor, trying
to get it exactly right, afraid he might lose the patient with a wrong
strike, unable ever to master forgetfulness: the necessary gift.

After two years, Bach's little minuet for Anna Magdalena sounded
like "The Parade of the Wooden Soldiers." After three years, a piece
finally came right. He called me thousands of miles away one night,
laid the phone on the black piano, and played the first two pages of
Beethoven's "Variations on Paisiello's *Nel Cor Piu Non Mi Sento,*" a
simple little tune over strummed chords, and the first easy variations.

"Lovely," I said. "Now let's hear the rest of them."

"Don't be a smart ass," he said, "That's ten years' work." He played
it again on the phone, half a continent away, while I felt in him the
lineaments of gratified desire. There would be no ten years, though
nobody needed to say that during this moment of spontaneous joy
in the hands.

———

I take my own hands to the black piano thinking this may be the last
music this lovely man hears in this world. Go out with the best . . .

I play a half dozen preludes and fugues from *The Well Tempered Clavier*, Mozart's A Minor Rondo, "On Wings of Song" transcribed by Liszt, "Jesu, Joy of Man's Desiring," "Scenes from Childhood." I improvise a little on "Tis the Gift to Be Simple," then play some last Intermezzos of Brahms, full of grief and singing in E major—slow waltzes out of a world no one in their right mind wants to leave, no matter its misery and stupidity. They all waltz inside me now: crippled Charlie and my father dancing with Auntie Ole, my red-haired mother who loved men so much, dancing with Michael and Alec, one on each arm. Weeping solves nothing now, so I suck in my breath, doing my best to make the black piano sing.

After Brahms, I think—what next?, begin browsing through Beethoven. Here's his own copy: fingering and directions for these variations penciled in with circles above the *i* in his fussy hand, more used to prescriptions and lists than words like *dolce, espressivo, cantando, appassionato.* I play the variations carefully as if they were a masterpiece. They are not. Only a lovely trifle, but this, too, like any small moment gives you the universe if you attend to it. At the end, I rise to go to his bed, not too sure he has heard anything at all. "And that, good doctor, is what it sounds like."

He opens his eyes. "Beautiful," he says, and does not call me a smart ass. After he goes, a day or two later, I find out he's willed me the black piano. I'm left to wonder: what music will it make now?

1700 36TH AVENUE

Your huge house was a curse.
Its many rooms allowed you
never to prune your life;
the house saved everything:
fifteen-year-old icebox notes
from your pilot lover: "Mike,
I'll make the cake tonight.
Get butter, Love Jimmy";
a beer coaster from Waterton,
Alberta, signed by John Allen
and twenty drunk roisterers;
a postcard from me with
a poem I'd forgotten writing;
a thousand negatives
for photos never again to be
developed on this planet;
an empty tin box with a note
from mother taped to the lid:
"These are your favorite
chocolate chips. Love . . ."
You must have thought,
like all of us, that if
these objects of your life
still lived in the back room,
you could visit them any time

you wanted, and then your life
would never disappear behind
you like a boat wake, yet
there you are in
a plastic bag on the fireplace
while we sit throwing, throwing,
telling stories, weeping,
imagining this big house
stripped, cleaned, Lysoled,
no dust or mildew left,
no pack rat ghosts
to pace it in the dark.

LEMON PIE

For your last Thanksgiving in Minneota I invited half the universe,
Holm's single-handed feed-the-hungry, stuff-the-lonesome-stranger
with turkey and giblets and pie. Already death had winked at you
once or twice from behind its shadowy curtain.

My neighbors pitched in with gravy, bread, and labor. Thursday
      morning
Tom brought lemon pies, steaming, acid-sweet smell,
majestic meringues, soaring peaks of beaten egg white.
On the table cooling, you smelled them, found a fork,
and, a mischievous sweet-toothed boy, were set to violate a hot
      meringue,
when I walked in and said, sharp of voice, "Get the hell out of there!
Those hot pies will be ruined if you dig into them."

"So what?" You shot me an insulted look. "They're only pies.
Eat them yourself." You skulked out into the morning. Toward night
your snit evaporated, and you resumed your usual grace and humor.
By then I'd grown my guilty conscience, remembering
that you lived under sentence of impending death.

I should have kept my mouth shut, one nagging inner voice
said to another, watched you put an entire hot lemon pie
into your gullet. What a hard business being human—
all we know and remember shadows every simple act.

The next Thanksgiving you lay close to death, all food
loathsome, indigestible. Kept half alive with cans
of glutinous Ensure, we made a lemon pie to tempt you
into one more small pleasure, but you impaled
the pie with a fork, left it standing upright in the meringue,
and turned away, lost to all joy.

We are who we are until we aren't anything anymore but air.
I carry that steaming pie to my own grave, offering it to you
over and over again, atonement. I hear your wry voice
saying, as it said so often: "Eat dessert first; life is short and uncertain."

LIGHTNING

for Phyllis Yoshida

You were a nervous man with a calm cat,
Lightning, whose attack mode
consisted of slowly raising one eyelid
or twitching a whisker as if it lived
in an atmosphere of pure molasses.
That cat respected gravity,
practiced only passive resistance to it.
An old friend who loathed cats, froze up
in their presence, liked him. He said,
"For a long time I thought he was stuffed;
then he shocked me and breathed."

Sometimes after a bourbon or two
you asked guests if they might enjoy
Lightning's new trick. You grabbed
torso and chest of sleeping Lightning,
held the tan fat fluff ball overhead
and waltzed and whirled through the kitchen
for maybe thirty seconds, stopped
and looked up while Lightning with
Republican deliberation stretched one
paw down, touched your forehead,
and held it there while we applauded.

O Lightning was a calm cat who had to be
startled into stretching. He slept at your feet
while you lay restless in your dying
and then like us, he outlived you a little while
but never did his trick again.

BEETHOVEN IN VICTORIA

Four Warsaw Poles and a Japanese woman pianist played Beethoven's
Wind Quintet last night in western Minnesota. Outside, a February
Alberta Clipper wind tried to bite everything alive in the throat,
thrashing it back and forth like the stop sign on the state road.

On the way home, I held the car to its course, like a ship's pilot in
a gale, steering into the troughs of the swells. The high beams lit
up the frozen black furrows to port and starboard. While the rondo
still danced in my head, an obbligato to the Clipper noise banging
everything outside, I thought of you, sailing on your boat, the *Cygnus,*
the last time I heard this music. Years ago we docked in Victoria harbor,
marooned by a July gale on the Straits of Juan de Fuca. What lovelier
place to wait out the wind with old friends? Julia and I strolled off
to the gray stone cathedral for a concert of festival music, a wind
quintet, with a piano, playing both Mozart's quintet and Beethoven's,
the loving godson's homage to that piece—his own quintet. The stone
vaulting of the old church carried the oboe and the clarinet and all the
rest up and over and down and around and over again. The wind blew
us into that music, so we gloried in it.

Meanwhile you and Don and J. R. had gone out to find the gay bar
listed in your guidebook, so Julia and I stopped for a whiskey under
a stuffed tiger in the Bengal Room at the Empress Hotel, a grand
Victorian stone homage to some antique imagination of empire.
Thinking the three of you would be out till daylight finding rowdy

sexual adventures, we returned early down the swaying dock to the boat, the parliament lights dancing a jig in the black water. But there you all sat—drinking cocoa and reading newspapers, listening to the scratchy nautical weather report on the ship's radio like three old ladies after the quilting bee. Not much gaiety in gay Victoria? I inquired disingenuously. You said something sarcastic, then resumed the editorial page. I whistled the Beethoven rondo and described two elderly English ladies with sensible brown shoes gossiping in the pew in front of us. Someone thought of spiking the cocoa with Bailey's. We sat up late, laughing and happy, pleased with each other, the sea, and music.

Years later, I reinvent that night, reminded by Beethoven and this harsher wind; you are a few years dead before reaching fifty. But you are present, in my head, in this car, on a blustery night in Minnesota, almost palpable. We never touched; we were American men who admired one another, practiced mutual humor, generosity, consolation. I reach over to pat your invisible shoulder, then think: What is death anyway? You catch a newfangled disease that didn't even have a name when you got it, and it kills you. There is a hole in the sea where your boat sailed, and a hole in the table where your elbow rested next to a wine glass, and a hole in the middle of your black piano where the notes to Beethoven's rondo fit, and a hole in the lives of all of us on that boat that night.

Will imagination summon you back to the world of tacking and luffing and cocoa and remarks? You become the wind—coming and going as you please—invisible. If you think wind doesn't exist, watch the iron stop sign shimmy on its post; feel hair rise from your head;

feel the bite on your face. Or listen for Beethoven's tune, disappeared for so many years into the calm air in the vaulting inside Victoria Cathedral on that balmy July night, blown back from Poland to Minnesota in cold February to sing again. Gone in the morning one more time, it will make its rounds after awhile, like the wind and maybe like you, too, Camarado!

MAGNIFICAT

I have taken the text of "Magnificat" from the King James translation of the book of Luke 1: 46–55. The Walt Whitman lines interlaced with the "Magnificat" are from a poem first called in 1856 "Poem on the Proposition of Nakedness," afterward "Respondez!" and finally dropped from Leaves of Grass *in 1876. That was one of Whitman's worst editorial mistakes. The full text of the poem is worth finding by whatever title.*

Seattle, gray December;
rain slides off heavy madrona leaves;
the sky a giant battleship
anchored overhead.
In an elegant old house
on the eyebrow of a hill
a man lies close to death.
He recognizes no one anymore.
His friends wait in guest rooms
not daring to weep yet,
everyone's soul clotted
in a gray emulsion:
rage, grief, love,
nowhere to spend themselves.

A choir in town announces
the Bach *Magnificat* for Christmas.
"My soul doth magnify the Lord,

and my spirit rejoices." Maybe this music
will give me permission to grieve,
to magnify a little early.

Underage virgin and old lady,
Mary and Elizabeth,
both pregnant, both violating
custom, expectation, nature.
When they salute each other
babes leap in their wombs.
Unlikely.

The program says: the Magnificat celebrates
the way God turns the world upside down,
"reverses the ordinary,
disrupts the flow, inaugurates
surprising transformations."

In the elegant house on the eyebrow
of the hill the young doctor
lies eaten at, insensible.
Is this God's work?
An old question,
it will not be answered.

The music begins. It curls, laves,
exalts, weeps, thumps, celebrates.
Every two minutes a new galaxy

dances through damp church air
into the ears, then the body—
ribbons of stars, garlands of planets,
space full of nothing but light.
It unlocks me and I weep,
whatever good that does.

Let every one answer! let those who sleep be waked! let none evade!
Must we still go on with our affections and sneaking?

He hath shewed strength with his arm; he hath scattered the proud in the
imagination of their hearts.

Let that which stood in front go behind; and let that which was behind advance
to the front and speak;

He hath put down the mighty from their seats, and exalted them of low degree.

Let men and women be mock'd with bodies and mock'd with Souls!
Let the love that waits in them, wait! let it die, or pass still-born to other
spheres!
Let the people sprawl with yearning, aimless hands! let their tongues be broken!
let their eyes be discouraged! let none descend into their hearts with the
fresh lusciousness of love!

He hath filled the hungry with good things; and the rich he hath sent empty
away.

Let churches accommodate serpents, vermin, and the corpses of those who have
died of the most filthy of diseases!

For he hath regarded the low estate of his handmaiden: for, behold, from
henceforth all generations shall call me blessed.

Let nothing remain but the ashes of teachers, artists, moralists, lawyers, and
learn'd and polite persons!

He hath holpen his servant Israel, in remembrance of his mercy.

Let the world never appear to him or her for whom it was all made!
Let death be inaugurated!

Magnificat anima mea Dominum!

Let the limited years of life do nothing for the limitless years of death! (What
do you suppose death will do, then?)

Et exultavit spiritus meus in Deo salutari meo!

The music opens the flood tide,
in me who is so sweetly alive!
but does nothing for the dying man.
He does not hear
even rain sliding
off madrona leaves.

Past all grief now,
he is about to disappear
into music, light, a bag of bone chips.
Soon we will neither
watch nor weep over him
but sing him back
from the world of light.

The singers bend over their music.
It's stern labor birthing beauty
from this printed page of old
chicken scratches and Latin prayers.
The cello saws; the trumpet
sucks heavy breath, wobbles, wets his lips,
hoping to spoil nothing.

It's a mystery why one
note following another
sometimes makes music,
sometimes breaks the heart,
sometimes not.

Don't ask the reason.

When we explain music
there'll be no need to die
or no need not to.

Listen as long as you can;
sing whenever the right tune
arrives inside you.

SCATTERING ASHES
AT LAKE MACDONALD

In September we
gather to scatter
his ashes into
the cold Montana
lakes he loved so much.

Just past the season,
crags already dusted
with snow, dank rain
at the lodge, passes
closed by tomorrow.

Under umbrellas
a dozen assemble
on the flagstone ve-
randa to watch rain
pelt the plastic bag.

Maybe rain will re-
constitute the man
like the freeze-dried mir-
acles performed on
television food.

He looks like oyster
shells ready to go
to chickens, coarse grit
and ivory chips.
The lawyer opens

a bag of Krugerrands.
"He wanted his friends
to have these gold coins."
But they feel like lead,
dead in my pocket.

Now somebody reads
Walt Whitman. Two old
tourists look puzzled:
"Put the dead anywhere;
I'll be satisfied."

We dip cups of ash,
our own part of him
to throw in the lake,
open umbrellas,
walk down to the shore.

Somebody plays tapes;
his hero, Churchill.
"We shall fight them on

the beach heads, blood, sweat
and tears." The sky breaks.

Rain takes a short breath,
pale lavender light
leaks out under clouds
over gray water.
Bone chips break and splash.

Julia brings down her
box. Inside a ship
she built of bamboo
twigs, lavender sail.
She sets it drifting.

The little boat, so frail
we can't imagine
it lasting ten feet,
sails on and on as
dead Churchill orates.

"If men survive a
thousand years let
us deport ourselves
so they might say this
was their finest hour."

More bone chips splatter
in glassy water,
still wider orbits.
We have built your true
ship of death, old friend.

BUYING A STONE IN ECHO, MINNESOTA

On a gray November day, almost snowing, two old friends drive to
the Echo Granite Works. Outside, a yard of broken stones; half a name
here, half a date there, a try at eternity that cracked and went wrong.
Inside, a dirt floor, an oil stove humming, a pulley to lift the great dead
weight up to carving height.

An old Norwegian comes up, says "Can I help you with something
then?" What sort of help do you come for to the Echo Granite Works?

"We want a black stone."

"Yah," he says and waits.

"For an old friend."

"Yah," he says, "Where?"

"Not in a graveyard."

"Where then?"

"In a garden."

"Black?" he says.

"Black."

"About this big?"

"That's about right."

"Smooth top or rough?" he asks. "Rough is cheaper."

"Rough." I suppose he has to ask these questions here in Echo. It's colder inside the shack full of stones than outside in the north wind.

"This black stone in a garden . . ." he pulls at his pipe, digs a pencil stub out of his pocket, "What should it say?"

Now there's a question. "It should say a name, two dates, both known, and maybe a funny sentence."

"What's that?"

"Eat dessert first; life is short and uncertain."

He does not laugh. "One *s* or two in dessert then?"

"That'll fit," he says.

What needs to be said will not fit on a black stone in a garden, but none of us needs to say it; neither the two old friends nor the

Norwegian with the pencil stub printing careful letters on lined paper, two precise *s*'s in dessert.

He says, "Too late this year. The ground'll be froze up soon."

Spring is better, we agree, for setting the black stone in the garden, after the mud dries up on the field road.

"Set her in concrete?" he asks.

"Just ground." We may have to move the black stone in the garden.

"That's about it then." He puts the pencil stub back, hands us the bill.

"The estate pays," we say, "for the black stone in the garden."

"Give me a call," he says, "after the frost goes."

LETTING GO OF WHAT CANNOT
BE HELD BACK

Let go of the dead now.
The rope in the water,
the cleat on the cliff,
do them no good anymore.
Let them fall, sink, go away,
become invisible as they tried
so hard to do in their own dying.
We needed to bother them
with what we called help.
We were the needy ones.
The dying do their own work with
tidiness, just the right speed,
sometimes even a little
satisfaction. So quiet down.
Let them go. Practice
your own song. Now.

ACKNOWLEDGMENTS

These poems have appeared previously in:

"The Ghost of Wang Wei Looks at Skagafjord," "Bread Soup: An Old Icelandic Recipe," "Summer Light in Brimnes," and "Icelandic Recycling on a Summer Night" first appeared in *Prairie Fire* (Winnipeg, Manitoba).

"At the Icelandic Emigration Center in Hofsós" and "To Kristján Árnason" first appeared in *Ice-Floe*.

"Food Fight Duet. Sanichton, B.C." first appeared in *Grain* (Saskatoon, Saskatchewan).

"What Beethoven's Music Will Do to You" first appeared in *Minnesota Monthly*.

"The Man Who Threw Nothing Away" first appeared in *Great River Review*.

"Angels We Have Heard on High," "Water Tango in the Sea of Cortez," and "Ecological Anorexia outside Tucson" first appeared in *Pictures of Holm* (Tucson: Print Well, 1998).

"Playing Haydn for the Angel of Death" was first published by the Minnesota Center for Book Arts (1997).

"The Weavers" first published by *Ox-Head Press*.

"Künstlerleben," "Hallelujah at the Sioux Falls Airport," "Capitalist Music on Luoshi Road—Wuhan 1992," and "Thistles" first appeared in *North Coast Review*.

"Girl Eating Rice—Wuhan 1992" first appeared in *Weber Studies*.

"Official Talk in Wuhan—1992" first appeared in *Seneca Review*.

"An Early Morning Café" and "The Sea Eats What It Pleases" first appeared in the *Loft Magazine*.

"A Visit with Fred Manfred's Ghost—Blue Mounds, 1997" first appeared in the *South Dakota Review*.

"John Clare's Last Letter" first appeared in *Party Train* (New Rivers Press, 1996).

"A Note on the Door" and "Letting Go of What Cannot Be Held Back" first appeared in *Prairie Schooner*.

BILL HOLM was born in 1943 on a farm north of Minneota, Minnesota. He continues to live in Minnesota half the year while he teaches at Southwest State University in Marshall. He spends summers at his little house on a northern Iceland fjord where he writes, practices the piano, and waits for the first dark after three months of daylight. He is the author of nine books, both poetry and essays. His most recent prose book is *Eccentric Islands* (Milkweed Editions, 2000). He is working on a new prose book: *The Windows at Brimnes*, a long essay on what the United States and the last forty years of his own life look like when viewed from the windows of his house just south of the Arctic Circle. The view is not cheerful these days.

MORE POETRY FROM

MILKWEED ◗ EDITIONS
───────────────────────────

TO ORDER BOOKS OR FOR MORE INFORMATION,
CONTACT MILKWEED AT (800) 520-6455
OR VISIT OUR WEBSITE (WWW.MILKWEED.ORG).

Turning Over the Earth
Ralph Black

Outsiders:
Poems about Rebels, Exiles,
and Renegades
Edited by Laure-Anne Bosselaar

Urban Nature:
Poems about Wildlife in the City
Edited by Laure-Anne Bosselaar

Drive, They Said:
Poems about Americans and Their Cars
Edited by Kurt Brown

Night Out:
Poems about Hotels, Motels,
Restaurants, and Bars
Edited by Kurt Brown and Laure-
Anne Bosselaar

Verse & Universe:
Poems about Science and Mathematics
Edited by Kurt Brown

Astonishing World:
The Selected Poems of Ángel González
1956–1986
Translated from the Spanish
by Steven Ford Brown and
Gutierrez Revuelta

Mixed Voices:
Contemporary Poems about Music
Edited by Emilie Buchwald and
Ruth Roston

This Sporting Life:
Poems about Sports and Games
Edited by Emilie Buchwald and
Ruth Roston

Morning Earth:
Field Notes in Poetry
John Caddy

The Phoenix Gone, The Terrace Empty
Marilyn Chin

JOIN US

Since its genesis as *Milkweed Chronicle* in 1979, Milkweed has helped hundreds of emerging writers reach their readers. Thanks to the generosity of foundations and of individuals like you, Milkweed Editions is able to continue its nonprofit mission of publishing books chosen on the basis of literary merit— the effect they have on the human heart and spirit—rather than on the basis of how they impact the bottom line. That's a miracle our readers have made possible.

In addition to purchasing Milkweed books, you can join the growing community of Milkweed supporters. Individual contributions of any amount are both meaningful and welcome. Contact us for a Milkweed catalog or log on to www.milkweed.org and click on "About Milkweed," then "Supporting Milkweed," to find out about our donor program, or simply call (800) 520-6455 and ask about becoming one of Milkweed's contributors. As a nonprofit press, Milkweed belongs to you, the community. Milkweed's board, its staff, and especially the authors whose careers you help launch thank you for reading our books and supporting our mission in any way you can.

INTERIOR DESIGN BY CHRISTIAN FÜNFHAUSEN.

TYPESET IN 11/16 BEMBO

BY STANTON PUBLICATION SERVICES.

PRINTED ON ACID-FREE 50# FRASER TRADE BOOK PAPER

BY FRIESEN CORPORATION.